contents

Pages 2 to 25
SO YOU'RE STARTING SECONDARY SCHOOL ...

These pages contain loads of advice to help you as you take this important step. Some of the topics included are: leaving primary school well, facing fear, the first day at your new school, worshipping God anywhere, surviving Parents' Evening, relationships, and a whole lot more!

Pages 26 to 32
BIBLE HELP

Seven days of Bible reading notes to get you in the swing of spending time with God — the One who will never break His promises to you, will never leave you and will always help you.

Inside back cover
OTHER RESOURCES

It doesn't stop here! Keep digging deeper into God's Word and living life to the full with Him.

BIG FISH, LITTLE POND

CAN YOU REMEMBER WHEN YOU STARTED YOUR FIRST SCHOOL? HOW DID IT FEEL? HOW DID YOU FEEL ABOUT THE 'BIG CHILDREN' THERE?

Do you remember wishing you were eleven or twelve and leaving for 'big school'? Well, now you are – how does it feel?

One of the things about growing up is there are lots of people watching you and learning how to do it. Right now I bet there are lots of small children looking at you and wondering what it's like to leave 'small school' and go to 'big school'.

Before we look at the thrills, challenges and opportunities of a new school, it's important to think about how you are going to leave your old school. Obviously you will walk out of the gate, but how will people remember you? What impression will you leave them with?

You are now changing from being one of the 'big fish' in a 'little pond' to being a 'little fish' in a 'bigger pond' (unless of course you're six feet tall and look sixteen years old!).

So what does this change mean? Well, when you have been in a school a few years you know how it works. You know where everything is, who the teachers are, where you should be and when.

When you first start a school, however, there are a lot of questions still to be answered.

But 'little' isn't a problem. Remember Zacchaeus? Take a look at Luke 19:1–10 if you aren't familiar with his story. He was little. A small man in a big crowd. But he didn't let his size (or lack of it) get in the way of what he wanted. He wanted to see Jesus and he found a way to do it – by climbing a tree.

Even though you may feel small again, don't worry. Soon enough you'll know the school like the back of your hand – and in twelve months' time there will be a load of other people coming who will feel just like you do now. Wouldn't it be cool to be able to help them next year?

little fish, big pond

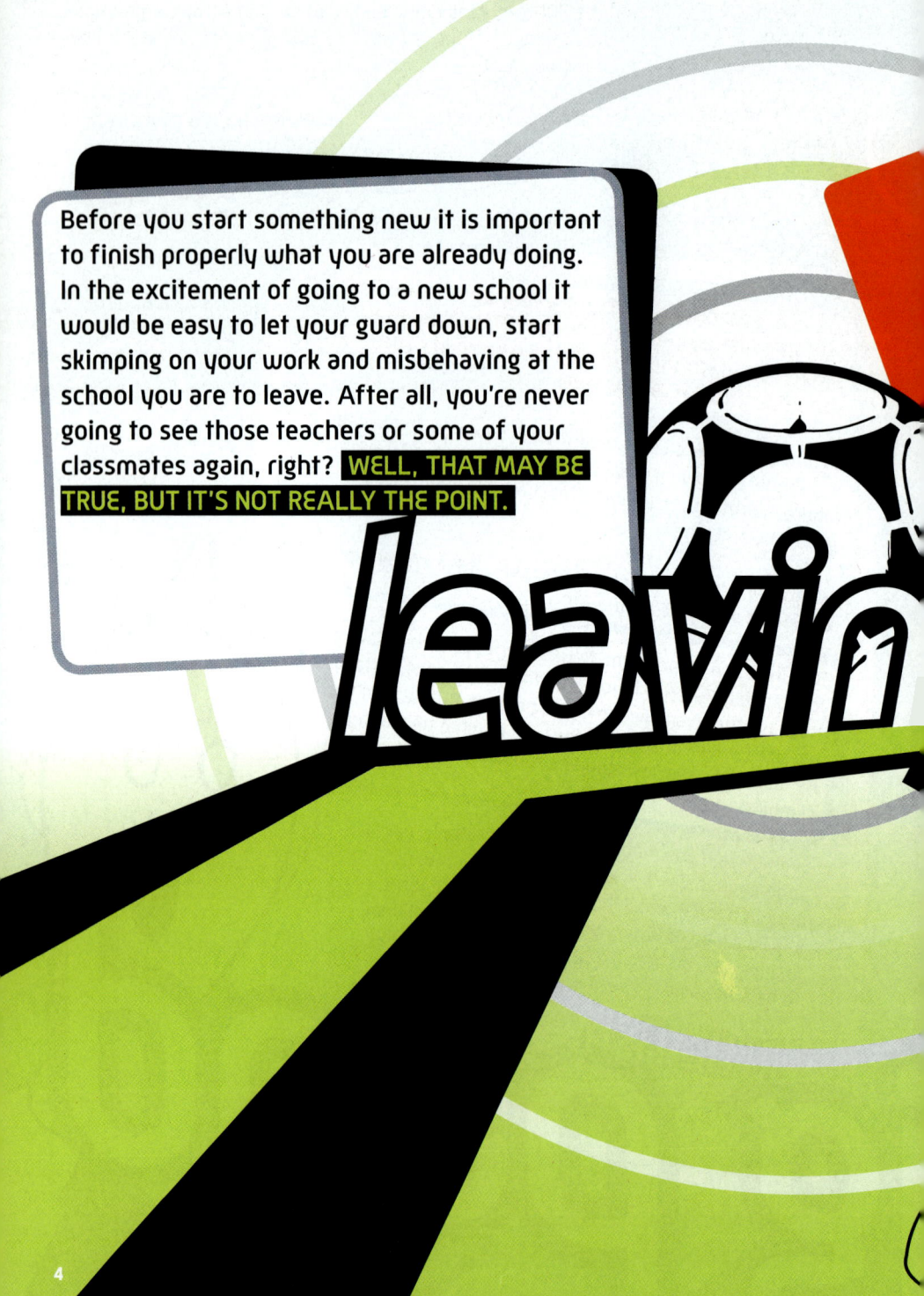

Before you start something new it is important to finish properly what you are already doing. In the excitement of going to a new school it would be easy to let your guard down, start skimping on your work and misbehaving at the school you are to leave. After all, you're never going to see those teachers or some of your classmates again, right? **WELL, THAT MAY BE TRUE, BUT IT'S NOT REALLY THE POINT.**

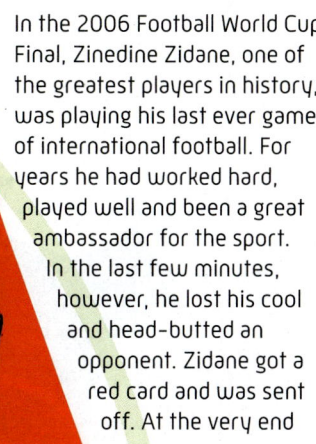

In the 2006 Football World Cup Final, Zinedine Zidane, one of the greatest players in history, was playing his last ever game of international football. For years he had worked hard, played well and been a great ambassador for the sport.

In the last few minutes, however, he lost his cool and head-butted an opponent. Zidane got a red card and was sent off. At the very end of the game, the competition and his career, it didn't really matter – the officials couldn't punish him by suspending him because he was never going to play again.

Sadly, not only will Zidane be remembered as the football genius who ended his career in shame, but he will always regret that he didn't finish and leave well. He left in a way that didn't reflect all his previous hard work, discipline and success.

WHAT IF I'VE ALREADY MESSED UP?

You may be thinking that you have already messed things up and you aren't known for being good or a hard worker but the opposite. Even more reason to finish well. Think about some Bible characters like Jonah, Samson, Peter and others. They all made huge mistakes and became known as losers, but with God's help they finished well. (Jonah's story can be found in the Old Testament book of Jonah, Samson's story in Judges 13–16 and you can read about Peter in the Gospels – Matthew, Mark, Luke and John.)

LESSONS FROM THE KOI CARP

YOU HAVE PROBABLY SEEN JAPANESE KOI (PRONOUNCED 'COY') CARP. THEY ARE FRESHWATER FISH THAT ARE OFTEN KEPT AS PETS. THERE IS SOMETHING QUITE SPECIAL ABOUT KOI, AND WE CAN LEARN A LESSON FROM THEM.

A koi carp will never outgrow its container. For example, if you keep a koi in a small bowl it will only grow to, say, 8cm. Keep it in a bigger bowl and it might reach 15cm. Move it to a pond and it will keep growing to 28cm, but put it in a lake and it will reach a whopping 53cm.

SO WHAT'S THE LESSON?

In order for us to grow to our full potential we often need to be put in bigger 'containers'. Going to a new, bigger school is an opportunity to grow to your full potential. If you were to stay at 'small' school you probably wouldn't 'grow' much more.

Oi, come ON, Move over

God wants you to reach your

full potential

— to become the person He has planned you to be. Sometimes, growing means we need to be in situations that seem 'too big' for us. But being in these situations is good for our growth; like some clothes, they are too big for a while, but you soon grow into them — and then out of them!

HELP! I'm stuck!

Facing F.E.A.R.

At some point we all find ourselves in a situation that makes us afraid; whether it's in the playground, at home, when we're late with our homework or trying something new for the first time.

Sometimes there is good reason to be afraid, but other times it doesn't make sense. Some people are scared of spiders, birds, small spaces or big spaces — there are even people who are afraid of buttons!! Fear doesn't always make sense.

How many times have you been really worried and scared that something would happen and it never did? You expected the worst, but it never happened.

ONE WAY TO THINK OF FEAR IS:
F - False
E - Expectations
A - Appearing
R - Real

Fear is natural. It's your mind and body telling you to be careful because they think something might be dangerous or hard. For us as Christians, however, fear is not something that should stop us doing what we know is right.

As a Christian you may feel worried and scared about something. There might be a real reason for you to feel that way or it may be because of a false expectation. Whether real or false, it's important to remember that Jesus is always with you and He'll never leave you.

Take some time now to think about what you might be fearful of at your new school, then imagine Jesus with you in these situations.

'Do not be afraid or discouraged. For the Lord your God is with you wherever you go.'
(Joshua 1:9)

"'For I know the plans I have for you," says the LORD. "They are plans for good and not for disaster, to give you a future and a hope.'"
[Jeremiah 29:11]

What a fantastic promise!!

GOD HAS PLANS FOR YOU! GOOD PLANS. PLANS THAT WILL HELP YOU GROW AS A PERSON AND ONE OF HIS CHILDREN.

Maybe your mum or dad or the person who looks after you tell you what they would like you to do for a job when you leave school. Maybe their plan is for you to be a doctor, teacher, nurse or politician. I bet for most parents what they really want is for you to be happy and make the most of life. But because they can't see into the future they don't know what will make you happy. Well guess what? God is your Father who knows you *and* the future; He knows exactly what is best for you … because He creates the future.

So wherever you go to school, whatever you do there, Jesus is with you and can help you through it.

THAT DOESN'T MEAN IT WILL BE EASY

When God promised the children of Israel their own special land, He knew it was going to be a good place for them to settle. He described it as a land of milk and honey — sweet and good. You can read the story in the books of Exodus and Joshua.

If you read the whole story you'll notice something else. Even though the land God promised the Israelites was good, the journey there and actually settling down was *anything* but easy. In fact, it was very hard. There were battles to fight, their own silly arguments, other nations poking fun at them and taunting them.

When God promises something He ALWAYS makes sure it happens. But the Lord doesn't always promise things are going to be easy or that there'll be no problems. At school you need to work hard to push yourself to learn. Similarly, God sometimes allows us to be 'pushed' in all sorts of areas of life so that we can grow more like Him. But it doesn't mean He won't come through and give us all that He has promised us.

On my first day of school I will...

Answer the following questions as honestly as you can:

On my first day at school I intend to
a) Bunk off
b) Spend no more time there than I have to
c) Be in the right place at the right time
d) Blow it up

During my first week of school I hope to
a) Find someone smaller than me to pick on
b) Keep to myself
c) Make as many friends as I can
d) Take over as Headteacher

By the end of the term I hope the teachers will
a) Want to throw me out of school
b) Not have noticed me
c) Know I will always try my best
d) Want to adopt me

It's attitude that counts

You have probably noticed that at school there are people who don't have to try really hard at anything – they just seem to be able to do everything, and do it well. There are also people who, no matter how hard they try, always seem to find things go wrong for them or they just don't 'get it'. Most of us are somewhere in the middle.

When it comes to school, it doesn't matter where you are on the scale – what matters is your attitude. Doing your best is all you can do, and is all that is expected of you.

'Whatever you do, do well.' (Ecclesiastes 9:10)

SCORES

MOSTLY A'S:
It looks like you're going to have a tough time at school. I suggest you have a long think about yourself and where you're going to end up in life.

MOSTLY B'S:
It seems that you may have some reservations. Ask God for courage and help. He will look after you.

MOSTLY C'S:
Looks like you're gonna be just fine. Remember, it won't always be easy – but a great attitude like yours will really help.

MOSTLY D'S:
Are you taking this seriously?

starting school search >>

One of the big challenges when starting a new school is finding out where everything is and making sure you are in the right place at the right time.

Below are hidden ten important places you may need to find at some point. Circle them once you have found them.

STAFFROOM	TOILET	CANTEEN
SCIENCE LAB	GYM	LIBRARY
BIKE SHED	OFFICE	MAIN HALL
CLASSROOM		

```
Z G D E H S E K I B W U
M A I N H A L L A P N F
O E C I F F O L X H M I
O H Y E E H E J D S U Q
R K M Y G C A N T E E N
F H T F N M A L L K K L
F T O E J S D L V O F T
A L I B R A R Y H B F R
T C L A S S R O O M O S
S X E S D G B V T P Y F
J A T M L S Q D F D F H
```

12

An 'urban myth' is a story that most people believe, but is not actually true. Most schools have urban myths about some Year Eleven pupil who flushes every Year Seven's head down the toilet, or the Head's particularly mean punishments involving jam and bees.

urban myths

There are thousands of urban myths about all sorts of things. One good example is found in the Bible. When Joshua was getting ready to go into the promised land, the children of Israel had heard there were giants there – huge and terrifying giants. Because the Israelites were expecting to see these giants they sent a report back saying they felt like grasshoppers and were afraid. This rumour spread through the whole camp until no one was prepared to enter the land.

At school you may hear many stories that make you feel small and scared. Truth is, school is full of children just like you, and the teachers are people just like your mum or dad or other adults in your life. Be careful what you believe. God says you are special and precious – that's no myth.

'I will never fail you.
I will never forsake you.'
(Hebrews 13:5)

Don't forget, you could talk to an adult about these stories to check out how realistic they might be.

You will have many hopes and dreams for your time at your new school. But in life, sometimes things don't turn out exactly as we hope.

Don't be disappointed if …

- You are in a different tutor/house group to your friends
- Other pupils get to be with their friends
- You don't make the school sports teams straight away
- There is someone else better than you at something you were the best at in your old school
- Your teacher turns out to be a right 'plum'

Unfortunately, disappointment is a part of life and hits us all. The important thing is how you deal with it. Every disappointment in life is an opportunity for something else.

Think of some of the characters in the Bible. Did they have it easy – Noah, Abraham, David, Job, Paul, John the Baptist … Jesus? No, they all had challenges to face – that's why they are great examples to us.

DEALING WITH disappointment

making PARENTS' EVENING work

For some the worst time of the school year is PARENTS' EVENING. It's the time when those that look after you at home get to meet your teachers face to face to discuss how you are doing.

The secret to making Parents' Evening bearable is talking to your parents or guardians throughout the year, not just when they get your report. Believe it or not, the vast majority of parents want the best for their children. Most don't expect straight A grades or you to beat the school 100m sprint record.

Sometimes it may feel easier to not bother talking to your parents. You may even think they don't understand what school is like. But they went to school once too (like, a million years ago) and can probably just about remember. Your parents want the best for you. They want you to be happy, they are interested in how you are getting on.

The Bible says, 'Honour your father and mother' (Ephesians 6:2). One simple way to honour them is by speaking with them, being honest with them and allowing them to help when they can.

You know, changing school is a big deal for a lot of people. That doesn't mean it's scary – it's just a big thing to do, but everyone goes through it.

It's often a good idea to identify a few people who you can talk to about things.

Think about it – every grown-up has been through it before. Sure, they aren't you and they may not have gone to the school you're going to; life is different now. But you'll probably find they learned a few lessons along the way that might help you.

history lessons

Q & As

FIND THREE OLDER PEOPLE AND ASK THEM THE FOLLOWING FIVE QUESTIONS:
(I suggest you ask a parent/guardian, a youth leader or someone in your youth group who's a few years older then you, and a member of your church who is over sixty.)

1. What did you like most at school?

2. What did you dislike most?

3. What helped you deal with what you didn't like?

4. What would be the best advice you could give me?

5. What would you do differently if you went through changing schools again?

Although the people you questioned have all changed schools before, none of them have changed to the school you are going to with the same pupils and teachers. Of course it was different then (that doesn't mean it was easier – just different), but there are still good lessons to be learnt from their experience. These people can't go into school with you, but you know what? … The Lord can. Jesus promised that He would never leave us. He is always there with us, knowing how we feel and ready to help.

'Give all your worries and cares to God, for he cares about what happens to you.' (1 Peter 5:7)

So you know that you're going to have more work at your new school and it is going to be harder. More homework, more exams, more coursework, more demands ... how depressing!! There's an old saying, **'WORK HARD AND PLAY HARD.'**

GO clubbing

With the harder work that you're going to have, it's a good idea to make sure you also have lots of ways to enjoy yourself (assuming you don't like hard work — maybe you do!). Sure, you could just go home at the end of the day and get on the computer or veg out in front of the TV, but sometimes these things don't actually help you to relax.

When you work hard you need to have some ways to blow off steam — you could do this through physical activities; for example, you could join some sports clubs. Or you could be more social, and meet up with friends to chat.

Joining one or two clubs can really help your start at school go well. Clubs help you meet new people and make new friends, give you new hobbies, interests and experiences.

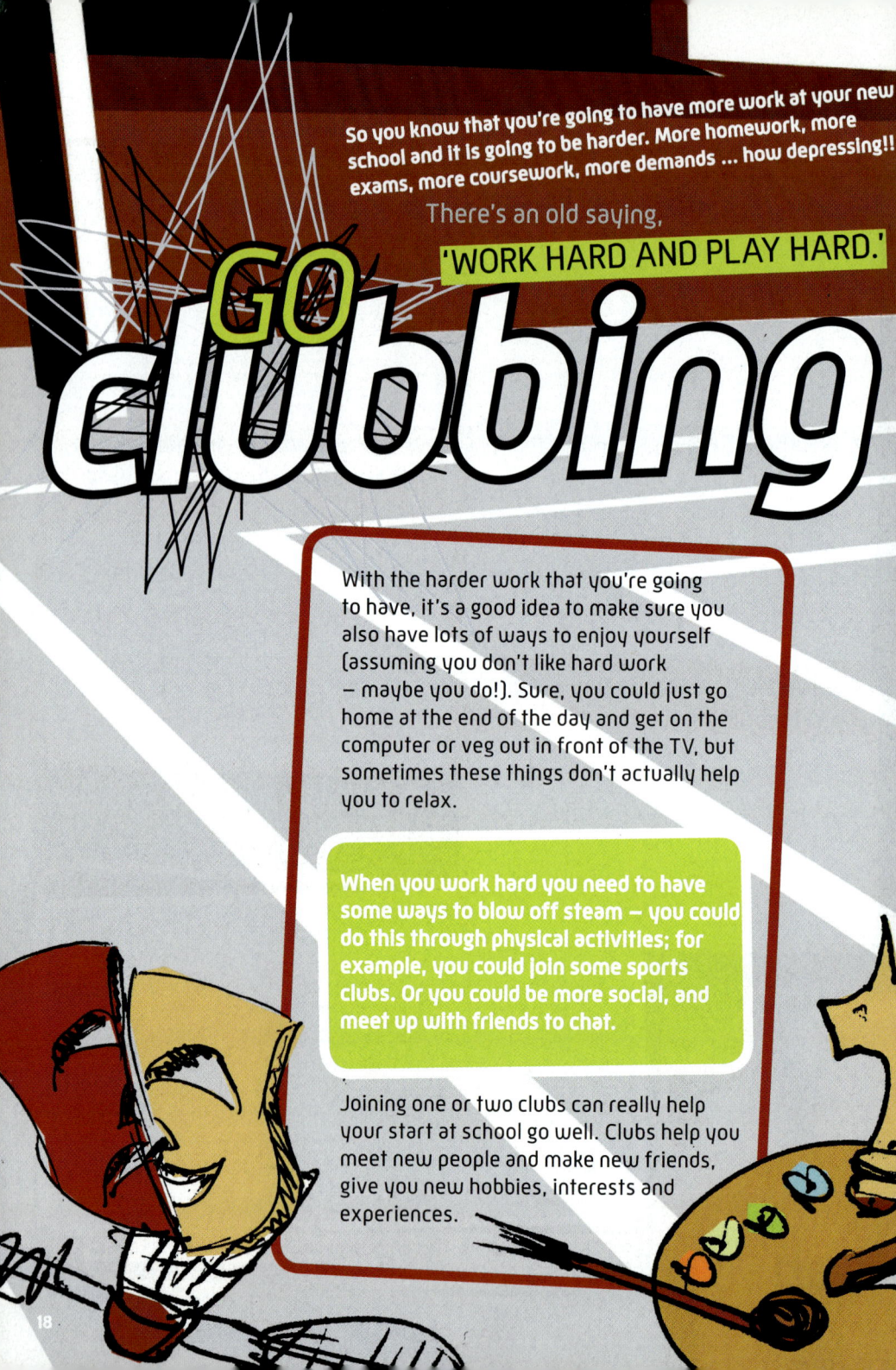

Christian Union

If your school has a Christian Union or club for Christians to meet together then join as soon as you can. It is really encouraging to get to know other people who believe in Jesus as you do and to be able to pray with them.

If you're not sure whether your school has a CU, you could always find someone at church who goes to your school and ask them. Of course, if there isn't one, you could always get a few friends together and start one yourself.

'And let us not neglect our meeting together, as some people do, but encourage ... each other ...'
(Hebrews 10:25)

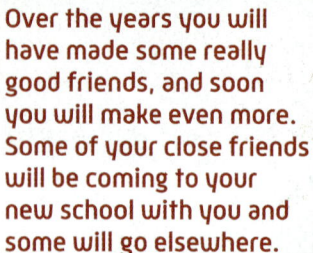

Over the years you will have made some really good friends, and soon you will make even more. Some of your close friends will be coming to your new school with you and some will go elsewhere.

On your last day of school and before the long summer holidays, you will say goodbye. Your classmates may take photos, sign T-shirts and books with kind messages of friendship, and some (probably girls) will cry. Many will feel a strange mixture of happiness and sadness.

This is a natural part of life – friends do come and go. Very few friends remain your 'best friends' for life – it's just impossible to stay in touch with everyone, but that's OK. Moving on to a new school is a chance to lose some friendships that you know in your heart aren't good for you and don't honour God – take the opportunity. It sounds harsh, but it's a real part of life. Some people just aren't good for you. It doesn't mean that they are bad people; it's just, when together, you bring out the worst and not the best in each other. It's also a chance to make some new, fresh friendships that will be good for you ...

relationships

never judge a book

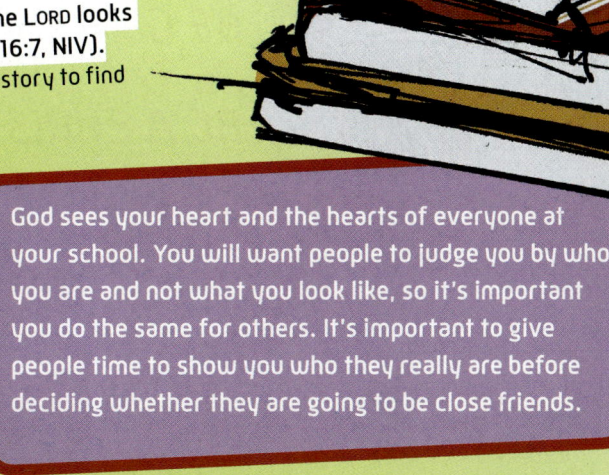

Whenever you start something new, whether a school, a club or later on in life a new job, you will meet new people. You will often find yourself talking to or being with people you don't know.

There is an old saying: 'Never judge a book by its cover.' This is worth remembering. It's all too easy to look at someone and instantly decide what you think of them, never actually giving them a chance to show you who they really are.

In the Bible God told Samuel to go to the house of a man called Jesse to choose one of his sons to be king of Israel. Samuel looked at the oldest brother and thought it must be him. But God said, 'Man looks at the outward appearance, but the LORD looks at the heart' (1 Samuel 16:7, NIV). Have a look at the whole story to find out what happened.

God sees your heart and the hearts of everyone at your school. You will want people to judge you by who you are and not what you look like, so it's important you do the same for others. It's important to give people time to show you who they really are before deciding whether they are going to be close friends.

choose carefully

It's natural to be nervous on your first day at 'big school'. After all, it's not something you do every day and there are a lot of questions you may have buzzing around your head.

When people are nervous they tend to stick to what is familiar or easy instead of holding out and seeing what new opportunities there might be.

We talked earlier about taking the opportunity to lose 'unhelpful' friends, so now it's time to think about what sort of new friends you want to make.

A NEW FRIEND NEEDS TO ...
(put the following in order of importance):

- [ ] BE COOL
- [ ] BE POPULAR
- [ ] BE KIND
- [ ] BE GENUINE
- [ ] BE THE SAME AS ME
- [ ] BE A CHRISTIAN LIKE ME

You may find there will be a lot of people who you will call a friend, but you need to take your time deciding who is going to be a 'close' friend. Close friends influence you, so it's important to make sure they influence you in a way that is good for you and that God would approve of.

school IS A PLACE OF worship

The title above may seem a bit weird, but it's true. Well-known (and very cool) worship leader Tim Hughes says, 'Everything we do that brings Him [God] glory is worship.'

Did you know that you can bring glory to God in anything? You see, when people know that you behave a certain way because of what you believe, that brings God glory — that's WORSHIP.

Here are some ideas of ways you can worship God at school:

- Don't bad-mouth your friends
- Help the unpopular people
- Show respect to your teachers

See if you can think of any more:

- ....
- ....
- ....

If you read Genesis chapter 1 in your Bible you will notice that God created the world to have 'order'. Think about nature, time, seasons, the human body, your pattern of eating and sleeping – everything has order. We order TV schedules, and number magazine pages so we can understand them.

Human beings cope best when things are ordered and running like clockwork. That's why you have a timetable at school, a homework diary and bells for lesson changes.

One of the keys to success in anything is forming a routine – one that runs like clockwork. You may find it helpful to think about setting up a daily routine so you get the balance of study, play and rest right.

Of course, don't forget to set aside a little time for talking to and reading about the God who created the world and knows how life works best.

DISCIPLINE, TRADITION AND HABITS

Setting aside time to pray and read the Bible will really help you keep your relationship with Jesus going strong. Some people think you don't need to do these things every day. In one sense you don't – there isn't an eleventh commandment that says, **'Thou shalt read the Bible every day.'**

However, making a habit of spending time with God will improve every area of your life – it has to. He made life, so involving Him is a really smart thing to do.

Forming a good habit is easy. First start with a discipline. A discipline is something you force yourself to do. You have to work at it.

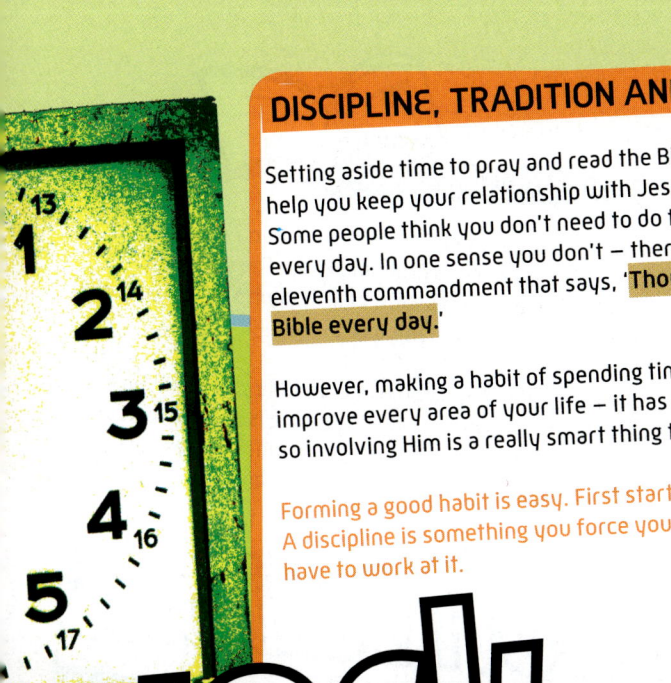

That discipline will become a tradition. A tradition is something that you feel you should do and you feel uneasy if you miss doing it.

This tradition will soon become a habit. Something you HAVE to do, you can't help it. You'd do anything to make sure it happens.

Why not concentrate on getting into a discipline, a tradition and then a habit of doing your homework, exercising and, most importantly, spending some time with Jesus every day. The next few pages of Bible notes will help you get started …

READ: MATTHEW 7:24–27

You probably know this story well (if you've been to Sunday school you probably know the song and actions!!). Sometimes with well-known stories we forget how powerful the meaning is.

Jesus explains the meaning behind the story. Anyone who hears and obeys Jesus' teaching is like the man who built his house on rock. The person who ignores Jesus and His teaching is building his house on sand.

BIBLE HELP – good foundations

THINK ABOUT IT

Life is like building a house. Ask yourself, 'Will I build my life on sand or rock?'

Right at the beginning of your school year decide to build your life at school on rock. Jesus is the Rock. Make sure that everything you do is based on Him, and when the storms (problems) come He'll keep you safe.

PRAY

Jesus, thank You that You are my Rock. Please help me every day to build on You and what You want for my life. Amen.

BIBLE HELP – actions speak louder than words

READ: MATTHEW 21:28–32

In this parable Jesus reminds us that words don't mean much when actions don't follow them. It's easy to say, 'I'll do my homework after this game,' but if you don't ever get round to it then you'll probably get into trouble.

THINK ABOUT IT

While you've been reading *New School – New Challenge* you might have decided to do a few things in a different way to the way you did them before – almost like making New Year's resolutions. That's great. Now you need to make sure you do what you say.

Write down at least three of those things below:

1. ....

2. ....

3. ....

Make sure you remind yourself of them every day until you are settled into your school.

PRAY

Lord, there are many things I would like to do differently at my new school. Please give me the courage and help to do what I have said. Amen.

READ: MATTHEW 16:24–26

Being a follower of Jesus is *the* most important part of your life. Yes – it is even more important than school!!

BIBLE HELP – there's more to life

THINK ABOUT IT

Even though being Jesus' disciple is more important than anything else in the world, that doesn't mean other things aren't important at all.

Put it this way: you can get everything in the world – the best exam results, job, money, fame and all that goes with it – but if you don't know Jesus it doesn't mean anything. When you die, all those things die with you.

Following Jesus gives meaning to everything else. A great job, money, family and happiness mean something more when you love Jesus. Instead of asking what can I get, you ask, 'What can I give away?'

PRAY

Thank You, Lord, that everything I have has come from You. You gave me my body, mind and talents. Please help me to put You first in everything. Amen.

READ: LUKE 9:10–17

The people following Jesus had probably walked a long way, listened to Him teaching for a long time and most had not brought food to eat. Only one boy had a couple of small fish and a few small loaves of bread — that wasn't going to go very far.

BIBLE HELP – take your bread and fish

THINK ABOUT IT

The boy gave what he had to help Jesus. What is it that you have to give Jesus at school? Talents? Time? Kindness? It doesn't matter how small you think your gift is, because when we give Jesus something He takes it and multiplies it.

There will be other pupils at school who will be touched and amazed by Jesus if you allow Him to take what you have and multiply it.

PRAY

Lord, I want You to take the little I have and use it for Your glory. Please show me what I have to offer and how I can give it to You. Amen.

the greatest

BIBLE HELP –

READ: MARK 12:28–34

Jesus was a revolutionary in every sense. His words and actions were often seen as 'different' compared to the normal thinking of the day. The religious leaders thought they understood everything God had said in the past, but Jesus often uncovered new meanings. This caused those who thought they 'knew it all' to become confused, jealous and even angry.

THINK ABOUT IT

The expert in the law wanted to test Jesus to see if He was a whacky teacher. He asked, 'Of all the commandments, which is the most important?' So, Jesus answered by quoting the teaching of Moses.

The Jews had one main command: 'Love God with everything you've got.' But Jesus expanded this. He added, 'Love your neighbour as yourself.'

You see, Jesus knew the experts in the law ('Pharisees', as they were known) had a habit of saying they loved *God* with all they had, but they were mean and horrible to everyone else. As far as Jesus is concerned, loving God and loving people go together.

PRAY

Lord, help me to love You with everything I have and love my school mates as well. Amen.

READ: LUKE 10:29–37

On page 30 we read about the conversation Jesus had with a religious expert in the law. In the reading today another expert (or perhaps the same one) is trying to catch Jesus out by asking more awkward questions:
SO, WHO'S MY NEIGHBOUR?

Jesus tells the well-known story of the Good Samaritan (it wasn't well known when he told it – he made it up). The man in the story liked certain people, but couldn't stand Samaritans. Jesus showed that the people we expect to treat us well can be a complete let down – and those we can't stand surprise us and go out of their way to help.

THINK ABOUT IT

If you claim to follow Jesus but are a bad friend, a bully or a gossip, then people will start to wonder whether you really love God.

BIBLE HELP – good neighbours

PRAY

Lord, help me be a **'GOOD SAMARITAN'**.
Amen.

BIBLE HELP – *fruit*

READ: LUKE 6:43–45

It's quite obvious really: good trees produce good fruit. Apple trees bear apples and spaghetti trees produce … well, you know what I mean.

THINK ABOUT IT

Good people produce good things from their good hearts.

The apostle Paul said, *I don't do the things I want to do, and end up doing the things I don't want to do.* Do you feel like that sometimes? Now, if St Paul struggled with this, then you can be fairly sure most other people will. But, Jesus has given us the secret to success. If you want to produce good things then make sure your heart is good.

How do you make your heart good? The short answer is … you can't! Depressing, isn't it?

Well it would be, but the great thing about Jesus is He does for us what we can't do for ourselves. All we have to do is ask and He gives us a new heart. One that's pure and good.

I suspect each day Paul asked God to renew his heart so he would do good things.

PRAY

Lord, give me a new heart today; one that will love You and others. Amen.

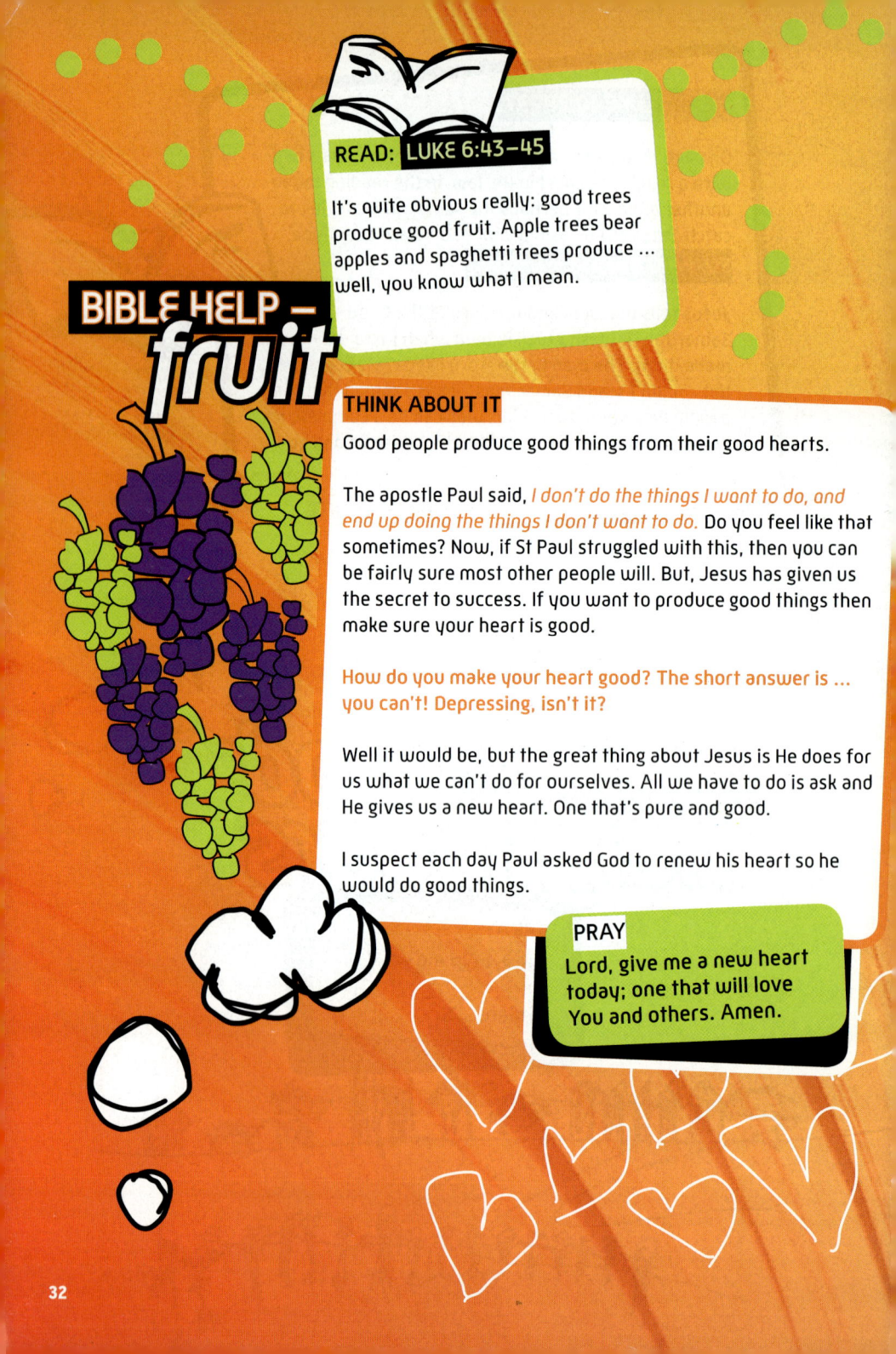